Bon Voyage

PACKING CHECKLIST

DATE OF TRIP: _____   **DURATION:** _____

TRAVEL BUCKET LIST

PLACES I WANT TO VISIT:

-
-
-
-
-
-
-
-
-
-
-
-
-
-

TOP 3 DESTINATIONS:

THINGS I WANT TO SEE:

MY TRAVEL JOURNAL

DATE:

WHAT I DID TODAY

HIGHLIGHT OF THE DAY

TRAVEL SNAPSHOT

DOODLES

MY TRAVEL JOURNAL

DATE:

WHAT I DID TODAY

HIGHLIGHT OF THE DAY

TRAVEL SNAPSHOT

DOODLES

MY TRAVEL JOURNAL

DATE:

WHAT I DID TODAY

HIGHLIGHT OF THE DAY

TRAVEL SNAPSHOT

DOODLES

MY TRAVEL JOURNAL

DATE:

WHAT I DID TODAY

HIGHLIGHT OF THE DAY

TRAVEL SNAPSHOT

DOODLES

MY TRAVEL JOURNAL

DATE:

WHAT I DID TODAY

HIGHLIGHT OF THE DAY

TRAVEL SNAPSHOT

DOODLES

MY TRAVEL JOURNAL

DATE:

WHAT I DID TODAY

HIGHLIGHT OF THE DAY

TRAVEL SNAPSHOT

DOODLES

MY TRAVEL JOURNAL

DATE:

WHAT I DID TODAY

HIGHLIGHT OF THE DAY

TRAVEL SNAPSHOT

DOODLES

MY TRAVEL JOURNAL

DATE:

WHAT I DID TODAY

HIGHLIGHT OF THE DAY

TRAVEL SNAPSHOT

DOODLES

MY TRAVEL JOURNAL

DATE:

WHAT I DID TODAY

HIGHLIGHT OF THE DAY

TRAVEL SNAPSHOT

DOODLES

MY TRAVEL JOURNAL

DATE:

WHAT I DID TODAY

HIGHLIGHT OF THE DAY

TRAVEL SNAPSHOT

DOODLES

MY TRAVEL JOURNAL

DATE:

WHAT I DID TODAY

HIGHLIGHT OF THE DAY

TRAVEL SNAPSHOT

DOODLES

MY TRAVEL JOURNAL

DATE:

WHAT I DID TODAY

HIGHLIGHT OF THE DAY

TRAVEL SNAPSHOT

DOODLES

MY TRAVEL JOURNAL

DATE:

WHAT I DID TODAY

HIGHLIGHT OF THE DAY

TRAVEL SNAPSHOT

DOODLES

MY TRAVEL JOURNAL

DATE:

WHAT I DID TODAY

HIGHLIGHT OF THE DAY

TRAVEL SNAPSHOT

DOODLES

MY TRAVEL JOURNAL

DATE:

WHAT I DID TODAY

HIGHLIGHT OF THE DAY

TRAVEL SNAPSHOT

DOODLES

MY TRAVEL JOURNAL

DATE:

WHAT I DID TODAY

HIGHLIGHT OF THE DAY

TRAVEL SNAPSHOT

DOODLES

MY TRAVEL JOURNAL

DATE:

WHAT I DID TODAY

HIGHLIGHT OF THE DAY

TRAVEL SNAPSHOT

DOODLES

MY TRAVEL JOURNAL

DATE:

WHAT I DID TODAY

HIGHLIGHT OF THE DAY

TRAVEL SNAPSHOT

DOODLES

MY TRAVEL JOURNAL

DATE:

WHAT I DID TODAY

HIGHLIGHT OF THE DAY

TRAVEL SNAPSHOT

DOODLES

MY TRAVEL JOURNAL

DATE:

WHAT I DID TODAY

HIGHLIGHT OF THE DAY

TRAVEL SNAPSHOT

DOODLES

MY TRAVEL JOURNAL

DATE:

WHAT I DID TODAY

HIGHLIGHT OF THE DAY

TRAVEL SNAPSHOT

DOODLES

MY TRAVEL JOURNAL

DATE:

WHAT I DID TODAY

HIGHLIGHT OF THE DAY

TRAVEL SNAPSHOT

DOODLES

MY TRAVEL JOURNAL

DATE:

WHAT I DID TODAY

HIGHLIGHT OF THE DAY

TRAVEL SNAPSHOT

DOODLES

MY TRAVEL JOURNAL

DATE:

WHAT I DID TODAY

HIGHLIGHT OF THE DAY

TRAVEL SNAPSHOT

DOODLES

Made in the USA
Las Vegas, NV
30 November 2022

60795231R00057